Once upon a time a little old man planted a turnip seed.

The turnip grew and grew into a great big enormous turnip.

One day the little old man tried to pull up the turnip.

He pulled and he pulled but he could not pull up the great big enormous turnip.

The little old man saw the little old woman.
'Will you help me to pull up the turnip?' said the little old man.
And the little old woman said,

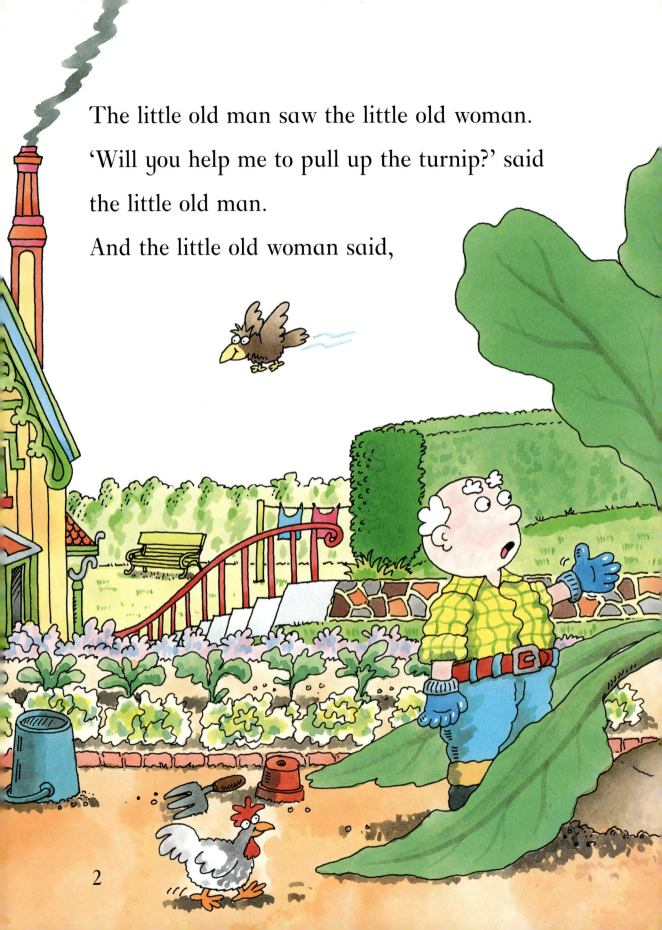

So the little old man and the little old woman tried to pull up the turnip.

They pulled and they pulled but they could not pull up the great big enormous turnip.

Then the little old man saw the dog.

'Will you help me to pull up the turnip?' said the little old man.

And the dog said,

So the little old man, the little old woman and the dog tried to pull up the turnip.

They pulled and they pulled but they could not pull up the great big enormous turnip.

Then the little old man saw the cat.

'Will you help me to pull up the turnip?' said the little old man.

And the cat said,

So the little old man, the little old woman, the dog and the cat tried to pull up the turnip. They pulled and they pulled but they could not pull up the great big enormous turnip.

Then the little old man saw the mouse.

'Will you help me to pull up the turnip?' said the little old man.

And the mouse said,

So the little old man, the little old woman, the dog, the cat and the mouse all tried to pull up the turnip.

They pulled and they pulled and they pulled, and then, **POP!**

Out came the great big enormous turnip.

The little old man, the little old woman, the dog, the cat and the mouse all fell over and they said,

The dog, the cat and the mouse helped the little old man and the little old woman to put the enormous turnip into the enormous pot. The turnip cooked and cooked and when it was ready they each had a bowl of delicious turnip soup and they said,